IMAGES
of America

DETROIT POLICE DEPARTMENT

POLICE HEADQUARTERS, 1866. Completed at the end of 1866, this was the first headquarters building erected exclusively for the police. It accommodated all the police functions at that time, including the newly formed Detective Bureau.

On the cover: The Henderson Motorcycle Company, founded in 1911 in the city of Detroit, built motorcycles that were the largest and fastest of their time, so it was no surprise that the Detroit Police Department took advantage of these locally made products to improve the efficiency of its Motorcycle Unit. In 1931, the Depression brought an early end to the company. (Courtesy of the Detroit Police Archives.)

IMAGES
of America

DETROIT POLICE DEPARTMENT

Lieutenants Donna Jarvis, Stephen W. White,
and Charles Wilson and Officer Michael Woody

ARCADIA
PUBLISHING

ISBN 978-0-7385-6199-8

Published by Arcadia Publishing
Charleston SC, Chicago IL, Portsmouth NH, San Francisco CA

Printed in the United States of America

Library of Congress Catalog Card Number: 2008928993

For all general information contact Arcadia Publishing at:
Telephone 843-853-2070
Fax 843-853-0044
E-mail sales@arcadiapublishing.com
For customer service and orders:
Toll-Free 1-888-313-2665

Visit us on the Internet at www.arcadiapublishing.com

CONTENTS

ACKNOWLEDGMENTS

The planning and preparation of this pictorial history of the Detroit Police Department was by no means an individual effort. As we began our research, we discovered wide-ranging support both from the department and from the community. The pride in their history and their hope for the future was evident.

First, it is essential to note that it was Ella M. Bully-Cummings, former chief of police, who initiated the creation of this book. She clearly recognized the value of documenting the department's history, and she should be commended for her efforts and foresight.

We wish to acknowledge the Detroit Police Foundation, the Detroit Free Press, the Detroit News, and Wayne State University. Without their contributions, this book would not have been possible.

Many colleagues also deserve thanks for their assistance. Among them are Deputy Chief Jamie Fields of the Risk Management Bureau, Commander Jeffrey Romeo of the Office of Civil Rights, Officer Alphonso Tinsley of the Detroit Police Department Graphic Arts Unit, and Officer Jeffrey Lemaux of Firearms Training.

For their valuable efforts, we also extend a special thank-you to the Detroit Police Department History Book Committee: Francis Allen, Nathan Anderson, Frederick Auner, James Bannon, Mack Douglas, Judith Dowling, Mary Jarrett-Jackson, Chester Logan, Daniel McKane, Walter Shoulders, Nathaniel Topp, and Robert Williams.

Finally, to everyone who enthusiastically provided guidance, support, and immeasurable input, we extend our gratitude. We are honored to have been a part of this project.

FOREWORD

The compilation of this pictorial history of the Detroit Police Department visually documents the foundation and development of one of this nation's foremost law enforcement agencies, from its first horse-drawn police wagon to the modern era of policing. Historically, it offers significant insight, not only into our accomplishments and sources of pride but also into some of our missteps.

Our history is important because it helps us to understand the present. If we are willing to listen to the voices of history, we can come to a better understanding of the past that can tell us much about the problems we now face. In doing so, we find guidance for our future.

The photographs in this book chronicle the undertakings, experiences, and traditions of the officers charged with providing police services for the city of Detroit, and I am privileged to serve as their chief of police. They are, in every sense of the term, Detroit's finest—men and women who have embraced many challenges and great adversity. Yet they remained committed to serving the citizens of this community.

How these challenges have been met throughout history is a testimonial to the professional men and women who have served as Detroit police officers with courage, integrity, and distinction. It is to them that this book is dedicated.

—Chief of Police James R. Barren, Ph.D.

INTRODUCTION

History is important. From a glimpse of the past, we can learn to value the present and gain a clearer perspective of the future. This pictorial history of the Detroit Police Department serves that very purpose. It presents a synopsis of events that reveal the skill, dedication, and commitment of those who have served the city as police officers. Even still, it identifies only a few of the many individuals who have stepped forward to ensure that the public's need for safety and law enforcement has been met.

The City of Detroit was founded in 1701 by Frenchman Antoine de la Mothe Cadillac as the settlement of Fort Pontchartrain du Detroit, and for nearly 100 years the protection of life and property was the responsibility of soldiers (first French, then British, then Colonial American) under martial law–type systems.

In 1802, Detroit was incorporated and the office of town marshal was created. Watchmen and constables were added in a somewhat desultory manner as the city grew, and when the Civil War loomed, military troops, under a provost marshal, provided police-type functions. After the war, there was a hue and cry by many citizens of Detroit who wanted to establish a regular police force; others, however, favored return to the old systems of town marshal, constable, or county sheriff. Many of these citizens who opposed the establishment of a police department did so because they feared it would add to their taxes. Nevertheless, the majority recognized the need for a permanent police agency and the Metropolitan Police Commission of Detroit was established in 1865 by an act of state legislature.

Beginning with 40 "officers and men" deployed from a central station, the department grew quickly in response to the burgeoning growth of the city of Detroit itself. The Detective Bureau was established in 1866. In 1867, a sanitary patrol was initiated to assist the Detroit Board of Health with nuisance abatement, and a Sealer of Weights and Measures was appointed. In the interest of expediency, rather than walking a prisoner down the street, in 1870, a covered wagon was provided for prisoner transport to the lockup.

The geographic location of the city—on the Detroit River across from Canada—also had an impact on the development of the department. The position of harbormaster, which had previously been a civilian appointment, was turned over to the police department in 1871, and a river patrol was established. A relatively few short years later, in 1888, harbormaster activities had grown so dramatically that a separate Harbormaster Bureau was established solely to deal with them.

As the boundaries of the city expanded, a mounted patrol was officially organized for the purpose of patrolling the outskirts of the city; and the police telegraph system that connected stations and Detroit City Hall was put into use in 1873. By 1877, the Detroit Police Department boasted a complement of 158 police officers that served the needs of the city's 125,000 residents.

The Detroit Police Department responded resourcefully to the growth in population and the expanded service requirements by continuing to adopt new procedures and methods. This innovative and determined philosophy has continued to be exhibited by officers throughout the department. By 1874, a rogues gallery had been set up to help identify repeat offenders. In 1877, one officer was detailed specifically to deal with juveniles; and a truancy squad was established in 1883 to assist the Detroit Board of Education.

In 1881, one patrolman was detailed as the dogcatcher and another detailed at the dog pound. However, it was not until a new dog pound was built on Campbell Avenue that ordinances were enforced. In the first six months of its operation, almost 4,000 dogs were processed at the pound.

Since its inception, several small stations and substations were added to the department's original central station building and lockup, and in 1884, a new police "headquarters" was erected at Bates and Randolph Streets, now the site of the Water Board Building. As the city continued to grow, substations and precincts were added to provide necessary services, and in 1921, famed industrial architect Albert Kahn was contracted to design a new headquarters building. At that time, this building was hailed as the finest, most complete municipal police building in the world. It continues to house the department's headquarters today.

Because of the city's expansion, officers assigned to foot beats could not adequately address the city's law enforcement needs. As a result, in 1884, a patrol wagon service was established with a new telegraph and signal system, which included street signal boxes.

The investigative skills of the department's Detective Bureau improved with advances in police science. In 1893, the Identification Bureau was established to assist the police in solving crimes. Later, in 1907, the department readily adopted the modern Edward Henry's fingerprint system to replace the Alphonse Bertillon method that used each person's unique physical body measurements as a means of identification

Before automobiles became commonplace, bicycles were popular modes of transportation. The Detroit Police Department found itself having to deal with the dilemma of speeding or inconsiderate bicyclists (known as "scorchers") on the roadways. In 1897, the first bicycle patrol officers were added to the force. They were known as "scorcher cops." They wore plainclothes, worked the downtown area, and their job was to apprehend speeding bicycle riders.

With horses, bicycles, and pedestrians sharing the same streets, traffic problems became a major concern of the Detroit Police Department. In 1909, the Broadway Squad was established and the Traffic Division was organized. Its principal duty was to assist the "decrepit old" and the "irresponsible young" across the street.

Motorcycles and automobiles also added to the traffic mix. Thanks to Henry Ford and his local production line that made automobiles affordable to the average citizen, traffic had become a major law enforcement concern. The department quickly recognized the maneuverability advantage it would have by using motorcycles for traffic functions and was the first department to use Harley-Davidsons for patrol. Detroit also became the first police department to use automobiles for policing, but only after Commissioner Frank H. Croul was able to convince the Detroit City Council in 1910 to appropriate funds by using his own money to buy the first automobile and demonstrating its effectiveness in police work.

The first stop-and-go sign, known as a mechanical semaphore, was seen on Detroit streets in 1913. By 1914, the first stop sign was set up; and in 1915, the first traffic signal was installed. In 1916, the first traffic tower, or crow's nest, was installed at Woodward and Michigan Avenues. Raised about six feet off the ground, it provided additional visibility for the officer who was assigned to operate the semaphore. The year 1916 also saw the first white traffic lines painted on the streets of Detroit; and it was Officer William L. Potts who originated the first three-color, four-direction traffic signal. In 1919, the Public Safety Bureau was organized; and in 1920, the Accident Investigation Bureau was established. The Detroit Police Department exhibited expert adeptness at dealing with traffic in what was becoming the automotive capital of the world.

The department led the way in police radio communications as well. In 1921, Commissioner William P. Rutledge became one of the first police executives in the country to foresee the use of the radio as a crime-fighting tool, and Detroit became the first police department in the country to successfully put a radio-equipped police car into service. The system was created by Officers Bernard Fitzgerald, Walter Vogler, and Robert Batts—all radio hobbyists. By 1928, the radio broadcasting system was in full operation.

Commissioner Croul also saw the need for better training of police officers. He started the first police academy on June 26, 1911, in the Central High School gymnasium. In 1931, a new system was created for the selection of police personnel, and advanced training courses were put into effect. And in the 1950s, the department instituted in-service training for increasing the knowledge and skills of officers already on the force.

In addition to up-to-date training, the department has endeavored to provide its officers with modern equipment. In 1956, it acquired two armored vehicles for combating "barricaded gunmen." Soon after, armored suits—precursors of bulletproof vests—became part of the police department equipment as well. In the 1970s, Detroit's officers began using battery-powered portable radios (personalized radio equipped patrolmen, or PREPs) to provide additional security and the ability to obtain immediate assistance and information, even when the officer was not in the patrol vehicle, and in the 1980s, mobile data terminals were installed in patrol vehicles.

Women, too, played an important role in the history of the department. In 1919, Josephine Davis was appointed as the department's first female officer, to establish a program of social adjustment with women who were taken into custody. Her salary was taken from the auxiliary, not the regular police fund. In January 1921, Commissioner Inches appointed Virginia Murray as director of a Women's Division, and 20 women officers were budgeted at a salary of $2,000 each. Their assignments involved working with women and children and tended to be more sociological in nature. It was not until 1973 that the title of *policewoman* was eliminated, and both patrolmen and policewomen were designated *police officers*. The Women's Division was disbanded, and women took on all the responsibilities of Detroit police officers. In 1974, Sergeant Cynthia Eggers, a 12-year veteran, became the first-known woman homicide detective in the United States. In 2003, Detroit appointed its first female police chief, Ella M. Bully-Cummings.

The Detroit Police Department has long recognized the value of good police-community relations and has implemented a variety of programs to accomplish that end. In 1954, civilian citations were established to acknowledge citizens who aided police in the enforcement of the law. In 1962, Commissioner Edwards instituted a three-point program. Its goals were to provide more law enforcement and more vigorous law enforcement; to provide equal protection of the law for all citizens and equal enforcement of the law against all violators; and to encourage citizen cooperation in law enforcement. Since then, the Detroit Police Department has instituted a number of programs, some local and some national, which are geared specifically toward improving community relations to reduce crime. Among these many programs are the Community-Oriented Patrol (scooter officers), Neighborhood Watch, Mini-Stations, Keystone Kops, the Blue Pigs Band, and McGruff the Crime Dog.

Detroit's use of the electronic computer was initiated in 1963 when the department purchased an IBM 1401, 8K system. Its operators were able to quickly pinpoint trouble spots in the city. The prediction of crime trends permitted the strategic assignment of personnel. A year later, precinct scout car territories had been reorganized as a result of crime trend statistics compiled by the computer. In 1964, the department's programmers developed the nation's first computerized modus operandi file that allowed investigators to match known criminals with various crimes. Later advances in computer and radio technologies gave officers in the field the capability to receive information and make queries on wanted persons, stolen vehicles, stolen property, firearms, securities, and boats. Computer use in law enforcement today allows Detroit police officers to increase both their efficiency and effectiveness. From video cameras in scout cars to databases dedicated to identifying criminals, to improved communications, the Detroit Police Department has strived to stay on the leading edge of law enforcement technology.

The Detroit Police Department, like agencies across the country, is challenged by increased demands with fewer resources. The dedication of the women and men who fill its ranks is unparalleled in this country. Yogi Berra once noted, "The future ain't what it used to be." He was not talking about the police department, of course, but he was referring to the concept of change. As we look back at these highlights of our history, we form a basis for looking ahead; and as the city of Detroit continues to evolve, one thing is certain: based upon the Detroit Police Department's history of professionalism and innovation, its commitment to serving the citizens of this great city will remain unchanged.

OFFICERS AT ATTENTION AT THE GRATIOT AVENUE/RUSSELL STREET STATION, 1870S. In 1873, land was purchased at Michigan Avenue and Ninth Street and at Gratiot Avenue and Russell Street, and station houses were constructed on those sites. The new locations were established on the basis of workload and population growth. The Michigan-Ninth Station served the west side, and the Gratiot-Russell Station served the east side.

POLICE OFFICER JOSEPH KRUG, 1872. One of the Detroit Police Department's first official uniforms is worn by Officer Joseph Krug in this early photograph.

One

LEADING THE WAY

CENTRAL STATION, 1865. On May 15, 1865, the very first Detroit police detail was dispatched onto the public streets from this central station, located on Hawley Street between Woodbridge Street and Bates Street. The lockup, however, was located in the basement of Detroit City Hall.

UNIFORMED OFFICERS AT ORIGINAL BELLE ISLE POLICE STATION, 1880S. These uniformed officers are shown standing in front of the original Belle Isle Park Police Station. At a size of 930 acres, Belle Isle Park is the largest island park in the United States. It was sold to the City of Detroit for $200,000 in 1879 as a part of a "Beautify Detroit" initiative.

UNIFORMED POLICE OFFICER, 1880S. During the 1880s, this was the style of uniform worn by officers of the rank of patrolman. It consisted of a hat with a small brim, a black long-style coat with eight buttons, a belt with copper or gold-plated buckles, a night stick, black trousers, and black shoes.

WINTER UNIFORM, 1889. During this era, officers adapted their uniforms to the inclement weather by including mink hats.

HORSE-DRAWN CARRIAGE AT NEW POLICE HEADQUARTERS, 1884. In 1884, a new police headquarters was built at Bates and Farmer Streets on a site known as Centre Park. All the central station operations were moved from Woodbridge Street to the new headquarters building, including administrative and executive offices.

POLICE HEADQUARTERS IN WINTERTIME, 1884. This beautiful image of police headquarters, which illustrates its exceptional architecture, was actually used for a postcard during this time period.

DETROIT POLICE DEPARTMENT'S BASEBALL TEAM, 1889. The Detroit Police Department has enjoyed a long history of participating in intramural sporting events to promote community relations and to encourage camaraderie among officers.

DETROIT POLICE DEPARTMENT HORSE-DRAWN WAGON, 1890. Officers used horse-drawn carriages as the first means of vehicular patrol in and around the neighborhoods in the city.

OFFICERS IN FRONT OF THE EAST CANFIELD BUILDING, 1896. After 31 years of operation, and departmental growth to a force of 472 officers, a numbering system for the precincts was instituted. There were six precincts and six substations that were utilized until 1910, when, because of additional growth, it again became necessary for the department and precinct boundaries to expand.

FIRST PRECINCT SQUAD WITH YOUNGSTERS, 1886. In 1884, the central station moved into the new headquarters building at Bates and Farmer Streets (the current site of the city's Water Board Building).

OFFICER IN UPDATED UNIFORM, 1880s. Toward the end of the 1880s and into the early 1890s, the patrol officer's uniform changed again. Although the changes were minor in appearance, it was the clean and professional line of the officers' uniforms that was significant in its time.

GRAND RIVER AVENUE AND TWELFTH STREET SUBSTATION, 1890. Officers pose in front of the Grand River Avenue and Twelfth Street substation. It was built in 1879 and was utilized to handle prisoner detention and service the north end of the Fifth Precinct.

HARBORMASTER STATION AT THE FOOT OF RANDOLPH STREET, 1890S. The photograph shown here depicts the original Harbormaster boathouse that stood at the foot of Randolph Street and the Detroit River. General Motors World Headquarters and Renaissance Center now occupy the location.

THE ROUNDSMAN AND CERTIFICATE, 1890s. This photograph shows the official appointment certificate of Charles Schnabel to the rank of roundsman. Roundsman was a rank similar to today's patrol sergeant. The 1885 manual of the department noted that the roundsman "shall promptly obey all orders received from the Superintendent, Captains and Sergeants." During the 1890s, the department did not officially issue any handguns to its officers. Instead, roundsmen and patrolmen alike were issued 24-inch wooden batons.

LADIES IN FRONT OF THE BELLE ISLE STATION, 1890S. Oftentimes the citizens would work with officers to beautify the precinct buildings. This helped officers to build better community relations.

HORSE AND BUGGY IN FRONT OF BELLE ISLE PARK STATION, 1890S. During the 1880s, the horse and buggy were an integral part of policing. Not until the late 1890s would the horseless carriage herald the coming of modern patrol.

THE BLACK MARIA, 1890S. In the early days, an arrested person had to walk the distance from the point of arrest to the station. It was not until 1870 that the department began to utilize covered wagons. *Black Maria* is a slang term for a police vehicle that was used for transporting groups of people who had been arrested. This Black Maria was used for many years to transport prisoners from the Woodbridge Station to the police court in the basement of city hall.

HORSE-DRAWN PADDY WAGON, 1890S. These vehicles were usually painted dark blue or black and much like the Black Marias were used to transport groups of prisoners. There are several theories regarding how the term *paddy wagon* originated. The most popular is that it was named "Paddy" (after the Irish nickname for Patrick) because of the large number of police officers of Irish descent and "customers" during the early years.

THE FIRST BIKE PATROL ADDED TO THE FORCE, 1897. In 1897, the department began its first bike patrol. The bicycle patrol officers became known as "scorchers." It was their speed and expert bike-handling skills that garnered them the name. The main purpose of these scorchers was to catch bicyclists that were speeding or causing a nuisance on the streets.

GROUP PHOTOGRAPH OF THE BICYCLE PATROL, 1897. As patrol areas increased in size, even the most energetic and motivated officer was unable to cover them in a single tour of duty. By 1870, the population of Detroit had increased to 79,577, which covered a span of more than 12 square miles. Pioneering ideas like the bicycle patrol, whose officers are shown here, became paramount in responding to the citizens' needs.

RUSSELL ALGER VISITS DETROIT FOR THE GAR CONVENTION, 1899. In 1899, the Grand Army of the Republic (GAR) held a parade to welcome home its newest leader, Russell Alger, a Grand Rapids native. He later served one term as Michigan's governor. Detroit police officers are shown assisting with this event. The GAR was a fraternal organization that was comprised of veterans of the Union army who had served in the American Civil War. Five members were elected president of the United States.

HORSE AND BUGGY AT BETHUNE STATION, 1899. In striving to better serve its citizens, the Detroit Police Department mobilized horse-drawn carriages in order to respond more efficiently to the calls for public service.

24

SIXTH PRECINCT AT THE DAWN OF THE 20TH CENTURY, 1900. Executives and officers gather to capture the moment of an era gone by. At the time of this photograph, the Sixth Precinct, located at Vinewood and Myrtle Streets, was only eight years old.

POLICE TRUCK WITH WOODEN SPOKE WHEELS AND CRANK MOTOR, 1906. The Sealer of Weights and Measures was responsible for enforcing statutes governing the operation of all weighing and measuring devices used in commerce and for responding to complaints on inaccurate weighing devices, short deliveries, and underweight or improperly marked products. This included winery measures, butchers' and bakers' measures, and weight of coal tonnage. This was the vehicle assigned to that detail.

First Police Car Purchased by Commissioner Frank H. Croul, 1909. Frank H. Croul was appointed as Detroit police commissioner in 1909 and served four years. He wanted to test the feasibility of utilizing the automobile in policing. Initially unable to gather support for the project, he purchased the first police car, a Packard, with $350 of his own money. During the first seven months of his experiment, the department responded to 2,235 calls for service utilizing the automobile. The experiment was so successful that the common council and board of estimates approved the purchase of additional vehicles.

SUPERINTENDENT JOHN J. DOWNEY, 1903. Superintendent John J. Downey was appointed in 1903 and held office for 16 years under five different commissioners. Superintendent Downey was the longest-tenured person to hold this rank, which is comparable to the current-day chief of police position.

OFFICER WITH HARLEY-DAVIDSON, 1913. The year 1908 marked the beginning of a long-lasting partnership between the Harley-Davidson Company and the law enforcement community. It was in this year that the Detroit Police Department became the first in the country to use Harley-Davidson motorcycles for police duties. In 2008, the Detroit Police Department remains honored to have been the first to put Harleys to work.

GROUP OF OFFICERS WITH A HARLEY-DAVIDSON, 1908. Modern advances in technology, like this Harley-Davidson motorcycle, made the patrol officer's job easier. This picture shows a group of officers posing in front of Detroit City Hall. (The building is currently used by Wayne County.)

DOGCATCHERS, 1909. Impounding stray animals was a job delegated to the department in 1868. In 1888, one police officer was detailed as dogcatcher, and within the first six months, 4,000 dogs were processed.

DOGCATCHER VEHICLE, 1910. The Detroit Police Department was not only responsible for the safety and welfare of its citizens, but of its animals as well. In most cases the impounded animals were either returned to their owners or dropped off at the precinct station until the owner could claim them.

OFFICER DIRECTING TRAFFIC AT WASHINGTON BOULEVARD AND JEFFERSON AVENUE, 1910. In 1909, the department instituted the traffic squad for the control and flow of vehicular traffic. The Broadway Squad was also organized in 1909 and was responsible for ensuring that the pedestrians made it safely across the street.

THE TRAFFIC TOWER AT WOODWARD AND MICHIGAN AVENUES, 1909. As the number of vehicles on the streets increased, new methods for controlling traffic were adopted. In 1916, the first traffic control "lights" were installed but were still operated by the officer in the tower. In this same year, the department organized school safety patrols, and white lines were painted at intersections throughout the city.

GROUP OF OFFICERS, 1910. By the early 1900s, the Detroit Police Department had begun to reinvent itself and redefine its organization. Officers were more uniform in appearance. The motorized fleet began to take shape and replace the antiquated horse-drawn carriages that had been used for patrol.

Two

SETTING THE STANDARD

THE BRASS ERA, 1910. At the dawn of the 20th century, the Detroit Police Department was on the forefront of technology. Early on, automobile manufacturers would use brass fittings, lights, and radiators to complement their vehicles, so these years became known as the brass era. One of the first automobiles used in police work in Detroit was the one at the Grand River Station in 1908. The driver is Patrolman William Schrimer. Alongside him are Detective Dave Thomas and Patrolman William Savory.

BIKES AND AUTOMOBILE AT BELLE ISLE STATION, 1911. With the advent of the bike patrol and the inclusion of the automobile in normal patrol functions, the department was well on its way to setting the standard.

POLICE BADGE AND DEPARTMENT-ISSUED WEAPON, 1913. In 1883, in response to the demands of citizens to protect them against civil unrest, the department began to issue handguns to officers. In 1911, the department, under the command of Commissioner Frank H. Croul, developed a police school, which was the first of its kind. It required that all new and current officers take courses relative to their jobs and that they obtain passing test scores. In 1913, the curriculum was extended to include quarterly instruction on the care and handling of the service revolver.

MOTORCYCLE OFFICERS POSING AT HEADQUARTERS, 1914. By 1914, the motorcycle had become a permanent tool in the Detroit Police Department fleet. The department began training its officers on a regular basis in the operation and handling of the vehicles.

THE FIRST TRAFFIC LIGHT INSTALLED, 1916. Although the first traffic control sign was put to use earlier, it was not until 1916 that the first traffic control light was installed. Officer William L. Potts developed the idea for a traffic control device for directing the increasing number of automobiles in the city utilizing railroad signal lights. With $37 worth of wire and electrical controls, Officer Potts constructed the world's first four-way three-color automatic traffic light. The light was installed on the corner of Woodward and Michigan Avenues in 1920, and within one year, 16 other automatic lights were installed throughout the city. Officer Potts was unable to patent his invention since he was a municipal employee.

TRAFFIC CONTROL TOWER, 1917. In 1917, traffic lights were still manually operated and controlled by the officers in the tower. Looking north on East Grand Boulevard, these officers remained steadfast in their duty to traffic safety.

THIRD PRECINCT AT DUBOIS AND HUNT STREETS, 1919. By 1919, the officers of the Third Precinct, in addition to serving citizens in an area about four square miles in size, were also responsible for protecting some 1,263 manufacturing plants. Also known as the Hunt Street Station when it first opened, this Eastern Headquarters was considered to be the most functional police facility in the country. During this time, officers worked 12-hour shifts with an additional on-call shift that was known as the "dog watch."

THE ACCIDENT INVESTIGATION BUREAU, 1920. In 1920, the Accident Investigation Bureau was organized to handle the large number of vehicular accidents that were occurring due to the increasing number of motor vehicles on the road.

FLYER WITH DETECTIVES, 1920s. Six detectives are shown seated in a 1913 Flyer, which was designed and built in Mount Clemens, a suburb of Detroit.

DETECTIVE BUREAU FLYERS, 1920S. The Detroit Police Department prided itself on using the most current and modern automobiles. Most of the Flyers in the department were used by the Detective Bureau and became known as the "Detective Flyers."

DETECTIVE SERGEANT WARREN C. RICHARDSON, 1920. In October 1900, Warren C. Richardson was appointed to the Detroit Police Department. It took several attempts for the young man to get accepted, but once he became an officer, he served the citizens of Detroit in a professional manner consistent with his personal character. As an officer, Richardson was astute and learned very quickly. He was fluent in eight languages and was awarded 17 medals and commendations for his bravery and commitment. On July 18, 1918, Officer Richardson was promoted to detective sergeant and became the first African American in the department's history to earn this rank. During his 26 years of service, Detective Sergeant Richardson not only fought the adversity of his time but undoubtedly paved the way for many young African Americans striving to make this city and department a better place for all.

DETECTIVES OFFICE, 1920S. In 1920, Detroit was the fourth-largest city in the country. Although the Detective Bureau was created only a year after the inception of the department, the skills that were developed in investigating crime set the standard for future officers. Also in this year the Women's Division was created. The women officers investigated crimes involving other women and their children, such as domestic violence, runaways, or disobedient children. Eligibility requirements were double that of male officers, in most cases women needed to have a four-year degree in social work to just apply.

THE GOOD FELLOWS, 1920S. The unforgettable cartoon of a little girl crying with her head on a wooden table while holding an empty Christmas stocking in her hand appeared in the *Detroit Journal* on Christmas Day of 1908. The cartoon was created by Tom May and provided the spark that led to the creation of the Old Newsboy's Good Fellow Fund in 1914. For the past 94 years, the proceeds obtained through the sales of newspapers and other efforts by the Old Newsboys have ensured that hundreds of thousands of needy children received Christmas packages. The slogan "No Child Without a Christmas" has been more than just a motto. Members of the department have supported this charity in a variety of ways, including the selling of Good Fellow papers, dressing Good Fellow dolls, and, in earlier days, by assisting with the delivery of Christmas packages. Shown here is Inspector Rick Williams selling Good Fellow papers.

MOTORIZED PADDY WAGON, 1920S. Although the people in the photograph have not been identified, this appears to be one of the first motorized paddy wagons utilized by the department.

ARMORED CAR FROM THE PROHIBITION ERA, 1920S. In 1920, and for the 13 years of Prohibition that followed, the department advanced its thinking and improved its equipment. Officers adapted to a time where criminals were becoming increasingly more defiant and dangerous. This is one of several armored cars that were used for raids on blind pigs and speakeasies. It is estimated that because of its proximity to Canada, the Detroit River, the St. Clair River, and Lake St. Clair, nearly three-quarters of all the liquor supplied to the United States during Prohibition entered through Detroit.

FIRST CONVICTION BASED ON FINGERPRINT EVIDENCE, 1921. This certificate commemorates the first conviction in Michigan's history that was based on fingerprint evidence alone. Prior to instituting the Henry Classification System in 1907, the department had relied on the Bertillon system of identification. Alphonse Bertillon, a French criminologist, developed a system of using measurements of parts of the body for the identification of criminals.

OFFICER ON AN EXCELSIOR-HENDERSON MOTORCYCLE, 1913. After the first few successful years of utilizing motorcycles in policing, the department gave the fledgling Detroit-based company Henderson Motorcycle an opportunity to prove itself and its product. Henderson Motorcycle was founded in 1911 and delivered its first motorcycle to the department in 1912.

HENDERSON MOTORCYCLES AND A HENDERSON MODEL G, 1921. Between 1912 and 1931, Henderson motorcycles were the largest and the fastest motorcycles of their time. They appealed not only to police departments across the country but to sport riders as well. Unfortunately, this company that began during the golden age of motorcycling did not survive the Great Depression.

POLICE HEADQUARTERS AT 1300 BEAUBIEN STREET, 1923. Since 1923, this building has served as the Detroit Police Headquarters and was designed by Albert Kahn, who was one of the foremost architects of the industrial era. The term "1300 Beaubien" has come to symbolize the Detroit Police Department in the same way as the headquarters of other agencies, such as Parker Center for the Los Angeles Police Department.

FOURTH PRECINCT OFFICERS, 1927. By 1927, the officers of the Fourth Precinct, seen here, patrolled an area that had grown to nearly 10 square miles and that was home to 115,386 citizens. The station was located on Scotten Street at Fairbanks Street. In 1929, the station at Fort Street and Green Street was opened. The Second, Third, and Fourth Precincts were recently combined to form the Southwest District and moved to a new facility located at 4700 West Fort Street. The facility includes a fire engine company, park and service center, and community center.

CRUISER ON BELLE ISLE, 1928. During this time period, in an attempt to dispel any confusion between gangsters and the police, detectives were chauffeured by uniformed officers.

THE NOTORIOUS PURPLE GANG AT POLICE HEADQUARTERS, 1928. The Purple Gang, one of Detroit's most violent groups of gangsters, rose to power quickly during Prohibition. Detroit's close proximity to Canada, and the almost limitless miles of riverbanks where bootleggers could stash their goods, made this a very lucrative time for mobsters in the city. They were feared by other mobsters around the country, including Al Capone. The Purple Gang ultimately self-destructed in 1935 with the deaths of its leadership.

FIRST RADIO-EQUIPPED POLICE CAR, MODEL T FORD, 1928. The department made history as the first police agency to dispatch patrol cars regularly by one-way radio. This came as a result of more than seven years of experimentation, between 1921 and 1927, with the fledgling science of electronics by radio buffs Kenneth R. Cox, Walter Vogler, and Bernard Fitzgerald, all of whom were Detroit police officers. The radio sets were finally successful in their implementation of a radio patrol car on April 7, 1928.

PATROLMAN WALTER VOLGER GIVING ORDERS TO THE RADIO-EQUIPPED POLICE CRUISERS, 1928. Electronics was merely a hobby for most people at the time Detroit police officers developed a stable radio receiver and antenna system. The initial system did not allow the police a specific band to broadcast on, so the system operated like any other radio station. The station was appropriately called KOP. Officers had to broadcast recorded music in between lists of stolen cars and missing children.

TWENTY OFFICERS ON A MOTORCYCLE AT DETROIT POLICE FIELD DAY, 1930. Officers entertained spectators at the Annual Police Field Day. These events began in 1927 and were considered one of the best shows of the summer. All of Detroit was invited to share in honoring officers who had gone above and beyond the call of the duty for that year. Funds raised during these events went to assist the "widows and orphans" of officers who had lost their lives in the line of duty.

Three

INNOVATIONS IN
MODERN POLICING

RIOT SQUAD IN VEHICLE, 1930. The department's enforcement of prohibition during this time was met with civil unrest. These factors prompted the need for a riot control squad. Much of its training was conducted on Belle Isle.

MOUNTED POLICE QUELLING LABOR UNREST, 1943. During World War II, companies sought out new employees to work in factories that made equipment and stocked arsenals that supported the war. With the promise of high wages, Detroit became a symbol of hope for many struggling families, particularly those from the south. As a result of these mass migrations, the overcrowded city experienced labor disputes and long lines everywhere, from the employment office to the grocery store and gas station. Mounted officers played a crucial part in quelling the unrest that broke out as a result of these conditions.

LABOR UNREST, 1943. During World War II, Detroit earned the nickname "Arsenal of Democracy" because the industrialized city made tremendous contributions to the war effort. Yet the cultural and social turmoil brought about by the rapid migration of large numbers of people looking for work in the plants created conflict in the labor market. This picture shows a white mob that overturned a car and chased the African American driver from the scene.

OFFICERS PATROLLING THE NEIGHBORHOODS, 1930s. Officer George R. Scott poses outside his patrol vehicle as his partner, Officer Theodore Robinson, sits inside the car at Hastings Street and St. Josaphat Street. During the 1930s, the department only employed 45 African American police officers.

LABOR UNION UNREST, RAILWAY WORKERS, 1940S. Once again, Detroit police officers were called upon to return peace and order to the community as a result of a railway workers disturbance. After the incident, an officer displays confiscated baseball bats like the ones used to damage the vehicle seen here.

ARMORED CAR, 1930S. While it may appear rudimentary by today's technological standards, this armored police vehicle afforded extra protection to officers confronting heavily armed individuals and was probably used when dealing with gangsters during Prohibition.

IRON MAN BULLETPROOF SUIT, 1940s. As technology advanced, the department researched the use of different types of body armor. This bulletproof "Iron Man" suit was designed as protection for officers exposed to direct fire. Its goal was to provide ballistic protection over a large area of the user's body.

HARBORMASTER BOAT, 1930s. Because of the city's location on the Detroit River, Detroit Police Harbormaster officers battled daily to keep pace with rum smugglers during Prohibition. This meant upgrading the boats to match the ever-evolving watercraft used by violators.

HARBORMASTER TROLLING ICY WATERS, 1940s. Even in the coldest of Michigan winters, the Harbormaster trolled the icy waters of the Detroit River to assist fisherman, locate vehicles in the water, or search for persons who may have drowned.

INFORMATION BOOTH AT CAMPUS MARTIUS, 1935. In the early days of motorized patrol, the department utilized a system that assigned two officers to a car. While one officer stayed in the booth, the other officer walked a foot beat. The booth contained a telephone, and the police dispatcher could contact the officer in the booth with a list of calls that required the officers' response. Today, with the construction of Campus Martius Park, this location continues to be a meeting place where residents, visitors, and workers can come together to relax, enjoy, and celebrate downtown Detroit.

Beautiful Star
1935.

BEAUTIFUL STAR, 1935. The personal steed of Inspector Perry W. Myers, commanding officer of Mounted at the time, Beautiful Star was one of the most well-known police horses in the country and was the lead horse in all the parades in Detroit. She was 24 years old when she died after serving the department and the citizens of Detroit for 15 years. The Elysian fields for this big chestnut mare is the city's beautiful Belle Isle Park, located on the scenic Detroit River.

OFFICER ENTERTAINS A LOST CHILD AT EDGEWATER PARK, 1937. Five-year-old Billy Stevens was lost, but it was not a dreadful experience. While the child waited for his parents, Officer William Lynn of the Petoskey station saw to it that he was comfortable and even offered some ice cream. The 20-acre Edgewater Park opened in 1927 and remained one of Detroit's greatest fun spots for over half a century. The main attraction was a rickety-looking wooden roller coaster and over the years was known as the "Wild Beast." The Detroit Police Officer's Association had its annual picnic at the park until it closed in 1981.

CHECK YOUR SPEED POSTER (MOTOR DIVISION), 1940s. One of the main responsibilities of the Motor Division was to catch speeding drivers. This poster served as a reminder to citizens that they should drive within the speed limit.

DETROIT POLICE MOTORCYCLE DIVISION 60 NEW MOTORCYCLES ON BELLE ISLE, 1937. The department first organized the Motorcycle Division in 1908 to respond quickly throughout the city. Here officers proudly display 60 new motorcycles.

MOTOR DIVISION, 1940. Officers of the Motor Division were trained in traffic safety and precision motorcycle skills. Officers are shown here lining up for inspection.

HARLEY-DAVIDSON SERVI-CAR, 1940s. The three-wheeled Servi-Car, introduced in 1931, became very popular for traffic and parking enforcement.

HARLEY SERVI-CAR, 1940s. These vehicles came equipped with a chalk stick used to mark tires of vehicles, recording the time the tire was marked. The advantage of this vehicle over regular motorcycles was that it had a trunk to carry cones and other assorted equipment used by traffic officers.

HARLEY SERVI-CAR WITH SIGN ON BACK, 1940s. The sign on the back of these vehicles clearly alerted motorists that these were Detroit police officers.

FORD DELUXE ACCIDENT INVESTIGATION VEHICLE, 1937. The Accident Investigation Bureau was assigned vehicles specifically to respond to accident scenes. Using the latest accident forensic investigation methods of the time, officers were able to determine responsibility for the accident and cite drivers accordingly.

NEW FLEET AT CHENE GARAGE, 1934. A new fleet of shiny police vehicles is examined by officers, detectives, and executives alike.

RADIO CAR, 1948. When the Detroit Police Department became the first to commence radio communications with its patrol cars in 1928, the system was a one-way, land-to-mobile system. By the late 1940s, improved electronics technology allowed for a two-way radio that was more compact, more stable, and provided both a receiver and a transmitter so that officers could send information back to the precinct. This 1948 photograph shows the police car dashboard with radio equipment, microphone, and police sirens.

MARCHING SOUTH ON WOODWARD AVENUE FROM GRAND CIRCUS PARK, 1940s. In earlier years, it was not unusual for the department to march in formation in various parades, as depicted in this photograph.

MOUNTED TRAINING DRILLS, 1940s. Officers of the Detroit Police Mounted Division display exemplary equestrian skills. In addition to police activities, mounted officers have participated in competitions and performed at reviews, field days, and the state fair.

POLICEWOMEN PRACTICE DRILL IN HEADQUARTERS GYMNASIUM, 1949. Officers of the Women's Division practice their drill formations in the police gymnasium in preparation for the scheduled annual Police Field Day that will be held at the University of Detroit stadium. Hundreds of officers and many professional entertainers participate in these yearly events to acknowledge the outstanding work of members and to raise funds to assist the families of officers slain in the line of duty.

DEDICATION CEREMONY FOR THE GRAND OPENING OF THE NEW CANFIELD STATION, 1948. On August 16, 1948, a dedication ceremony was held for the grand opening of the new Canfield station. In later years, this building would house the 13th Precinct and later the Central District.

COMMISSIONER FRANK EAMAN PRESENTING DRILL TROPHY, 1940. Competition winners stand at attention as Commissioner Eaman presents their team with the championship trophy.

PRISONERS BEING LOADED INTO PADDY WAGON, 1940s. Whether they were going to court or to the station from the scene of their arrest, this method of conveyance made travel easier and allowed police officers to return to patrol more quickly.

JOE LOUIS EXHIBITION FIGHT FOR CHARITY, 1938. Less than two months after beating Max Schmeling in a world heavyweight boxing championship fight on June 22, 1938, Joe Louis fought in a charity fight at the Michigan State Fair Grounds in Detroit.

JOE LOUIS WITH MAYOR RICHARD READING AND COMMISSIONER FRANK EAMAN, 1938. World heavyweight boxing champion Joe Louis is welcomed home to Detroit by Mayor Richard Reading and Commissioner Frank Eaman. Police officers provided security for the event.

TUG-OF-WAR CHAMPS, 1941. The contest of pulling on a rope originates from ancient ceremonies and rituals. The sport of tug-of-war in modern times has offered a friendly competition between various police agencies. This photograph shows the champion Detroit Police tug-of-war team.

DETROIT PISTOL TEAM, 1946. The 1946 department pistol team won numerous national, regional, and world awards for marksmanship, including the prestigious Colt Trophy and the police team trophy.

Four

BREAKING GROUND

DETROIT POLICE BADGES. This photograph represents the current active-duty badges in the Detroit Police Department.

CORA MAE BROWN, 1952. Cora Mae Brown was eight years old when her family moved to Detroit. By the late 1930s, she had taken a job with the Detroit Police Department while attending Wayne State University Law School. In 1948, she was accepted into the Michigan Bar. By 1952, this proud Detroit police officer had become the first African American woman to be elected to the Michigan State Senate.

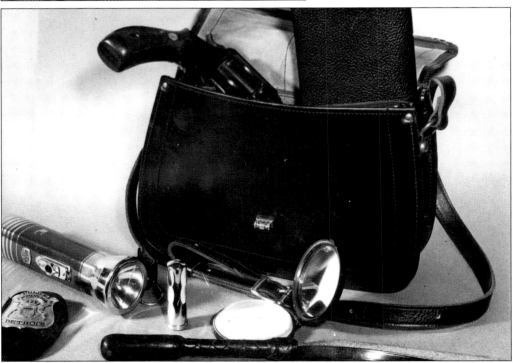

WOMEN'S DIVISION EQUIPMENT, 1950s. This photograph displays some of the equipment of members assigned to the Women's Division in the early days. The purse was designed with a holster inside to hold the weapons of female officers.

WOMEN'S DIVISION RESPONSIBILITIES, 1950S.

Although the Women's Division was created in 1920, its early history involved mainly providing social services and clerical responsibilities. Over time, their list of assignments grew, but women police officers still typically had to meet higher standards for employment. Members of the Women's Division interviewed individuals, processed complaints, and secured warrants. They also registered women prisoners and visited places where youth congregated, such as bowling alleys, playfields, and poolrooms. The goal was to prevent youth from becoming either victims or perpetrators of crime.

WOMEN'S DIVISION SHOOTING PRACTICE, 1950S. As sworn police officers, members of the Women's Division were required to participate in the annual firearms qualifications.

POLICEMEN AND POLICEWOMEN TRAINING AT ROUGE RANGE, 1946. Officers participate in the Detroit Police Department annual firearms training and qualification course at the range located in Rouge Park. At this time in the department's qualification program, officers who scored 60-69 hits out of 100 received one day off with pay while 70-79 hits earned two days, and 80 or more hits earned the member three days. It is not known when this practice started, but it ended before the 1970s.

STUDENT POLICE OFFICER TRAINING, 1954. Herbert White, an instructor at the academy for many years, demonstrates to a group of eager students the proper way to conduct a pat down for weapons.

DUSTING A CASH REGISTER, 1950S. By the 1950s, the department had become extremely proficient in the collection of fingerprint evidence and use of fingerprinting to identify perpetrators of crime. Smaller police departments would often rely on the expertise of the Detroit Police Department for assistance in solving crimes.

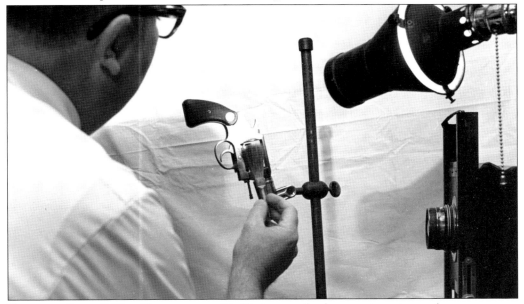

FIREARMS LAB, 1950S. The concept of ballistics goes back to ancient times when war meant slinging a rock at a fortified town. The modern science of ballistics functions to assist police in criminal investigations by allowing them to match a bullet to a firearm and determine the range of the shot, the materials the bullet passed through, and the path that the bullet has taken. Early on, the Detroit Police Department began to conduct its own tests on the weapons used in crimes.

DETROIT'S OWN UNTOUCHABLE, 1952. Vice Squad Inspector Clayton Nowlin is shown here on the street holding a bag of seized evidence. The other photograph shows him pushing a cart full of evidence to court. The confiscated items consisted of some 100,000 number slips, 10,000 bet books, and 100 adding machine tapes, which were seized along with 17 cars during a raid on an illegal gambling establishment. Beginning in 1940, Inspector Nowlin worked in the vice squad for 18 years. A *Detroit News* headline on January 7, 1958, said, "Nowlin Quits, Hoods Happy." The news report further stated that the inspector "was the bane of numbers of racketeers and gamblers in Detroit. He and his squad of hand-picked cops were known as Detroit's own Untouchables because the powerful gambling bosses could not bluff, bribe, scare or stop them in court."

EISENHOWER MOTORCADE, 1954. On October 29, 1954, President Dwight D. Eisenhower visited Detroit, encouraging citizens to vote and surveying the industrialized metropolis that supplied the war years. During the visit, Detroit police officers were responsible for crowd control and security near Cadillac Square.

EISENHOWER VISIT TO AUTOMOBILE SHOW, 1960. During a visit in 1960, Eisenhower toured the Detroit Automobile Show where he gave a speech regarding the impending election, global relief funds with the United Nations, and other topical issues. It was a state of the union address of sorts. Once again, officers were pivotal in ensuring the safety of both the president and citizens during the visit.

New Desoto, 1955. In 1955, the department continued its experimentation with different makes and models of vehicles, and the Desoto's V-8 engine seemed exactly what was needed. By 1957, with all the major highways being developed in and around the city, the department began to experiment with the use of radar to detect speed violators. The strange-looking box on the trunk of the patrol car is the radar equipment utilized at that time.

TUG-OF-WAR TEAM PULLING A TANK, 1950s. The tug-of-war team was one of the department's most popular sports teams. It won many titles and battled fiercely against one of its main rivals, the Royal Canadian Mounties. This photograph depicts a test of its strength.

DETROIT POLICE TANK, 1958. This vehicle, produced by the Ford Motor Company, was named the M8 armored car. After a specific request from Commissioner Edward Piggins, the U.S. Army modified the vehicle to make it more adaptable to Detroit's urban environment. Commissioner Piggins planned that the vehicle would be assigned to the newly formed "Commando Squad" to be utilized for civil disturbances and armed barricaded person situations.

Detroit Police Amphibious Truck, 1960. Michigan's frequently changing weather conditions and the numerous lakes, rivers, and swamplands that surround the area were the primary reasons that the department was persuaded to conduct experiments with the viability of this amphibious vehicle for search-and-rescue missions.

Lost Child or Bad Boy, 1960s. Although initially there were two other units organized to contend with juvenile offenders, the Youth Bureau was designed to encompass all aspects of law enforcement contact with juveniles. The persons in this photograph have not been identified, and the question remains as to whether this officer is dealing with a lost child or hardened criminal.

OFFICERS USING CALL BOX, 1957. Even after the invention of the two-way radio in the 1930s, officers found the call box to be a reliable form of communication. First installed in the early 1880s, the boxes remained in use until the mid-1970s.

SCOOTER OFFICERS ON DETAIL, 1960s. These scooters were introduced into the department as a means for foot patrol officers to cover a larger area. By this time, the downtown area alone covered 1.6 square miles.

FLEET OF DODGES, 1961. During this time, the department's fleet consisted mostly of Dodge and Plymouth scout cars. It was their sleeker design and heavy-duty engine that initially attracted departments around the country to these vehicles.

PALMER PARK BIKE PATROL, 1962. By the time this photograph was taken, 65 years had passed since the first bike patrol hit the streets of Detroit. Bike patrols functioned in areas where larger motorized vehicles had more difficulty in maneuvering. The Bike Patrol Unit had proven itself to be extremely efficient and a viable means to facilitate a closer contact with the public. Pictured here are, from left to right, Officers Richard Stokes and Joseph Syfax of the 12th Precinct on bike patrol in Palmer Park.

OFFICER DEMONSTRATING NEW PREP RADIO, 1965. Portable transmitter-receivers enabled officers to remain in constant contact with other officers and with the communications center, even when they were not in a patrol car. These devices were called PREPs—personalized radio equipped patrolmen—and provided for a fully coordinated patrol force.

SCOOTER PHONES, 1968. Within just three years, the technological advancement of the PREP radio was notable (see the size difference from the previous photograph). Officer Charles Johnson displays the combination microphone-speaker. It was reported that Motorola selected the Detroit Police Department to introduce its new radios, further emphasizing the department's role in innovated policing techniques.

DETROIT POLICE DEPARTMENT 100TH ANNIVERSARY, 1965. On May 15, 1965, the Detroit Police Department celebrated its 100th anniversary. This photograph shows Commissioner Ray Girardin standing by executive officers and their families after the commemorative parade. Also during its centennial year, the Detroit Police Department implemented a Police Community Relations Program. Eighteen hundred officers attended this extensive training program, which was the first of its kind and attracted national media attention.

DEPARTMENT'S CENTENNIAL PARADE, 1965. Officers from the Mounted Unit lead the way during the department's centennial parade. The Mounted Unit would celebrate its own 100th anniversary in 1993.

TACTICAL MOBILE UNIT AND THE PLYMOUTH FURY, 1965. This sporty model of the Plymouth Fury gave the department a slim and sleek performance look. It was used by the newly organized Tactical Mobile Unit and gave at least the impression that faster vehicles could respond more quickly to incidents anywhere in the city.

TACTICAL TRAINING WITH HECKLERS, 1965. During its history, officers of the Detroit Police Department have been responsible for bringing peace and order to the city. As a result, officers trained rigorously in tactical deployment so that they would be prepared to handle any civil disturbance.

TWELFTH STREET CIVIL DISTURBANCE, 1967. In the early Sunday morning hours of July 23, 1967, Detroit police officers raided a blind pig. Protestors gathered outside the location, and the confrontation that ensued was one of the most notable civil disturbances in U.S. history.

NATIONAL GUARDSMEN AND ARMY TROOPS ORDERED, 1967. Ultimately, President Lyndon B. Johnson sent in National Guardsmen and U.S. Army troops to assist Detroit police in restoring order.

DASHBOARD OF A POLICE CAR, 1966. The department initiated the use of "hot sheets" that listed all motor vehicles stolen or used in a crime. The information on these hot sheets allowed patrolling officers to quickly identify vehicles that were wanted.

ST. AGNES SCHOOL OFFICERS, 1969. Even before crosswalks were first painted on the streets, officers of the Detroit Police Department made every effort to ensure the safety of the city's children. In addition to providing crosswalk safety, assigning officers to a school also allows children an opportunity to get to know the police.

Mounted Officer at School, 1969. The children at this Detroit public school enjoy their extra lesson as a mounted officer teaches them about safety and stranger awareness.

Super Cop, or Wishful Thinking, 1970. On January 5, 1970, Lieutenant Frank Blount of the Community-Oriented Policing Unit tried on a futuristic piece of equipment that some believed would propel policing into a Dick Tracy–type of law enforcement environment and have officers flying around the city on patrol and responding to citizen calls for service. Instead, the closest thing that has developed is the two-wheeled electric Segway that provides an environmentally friendly transportation alternative but is a far cry from the envisioned flying machine.

Being a cop is more than just a gig.

Detroit Police Recruiting
224-4333

MAYOR ROMAN GRIBBS WORKS TO RECRUIT AFRICAN AMERICAN MEN, 1970. By 1970, the city's population was nearly 45 percent African American, and yet there were fewer than 7 percent African American officers in the department. To make the department more representative of the population, Mayor Roman Gribbs actively recruited African Americans.

There are never enough big men to go around.

Stop by Detroit
Police Headquarters.

Five

CHANGING WITH THE TIMES

SOME CALL HIM PIG, 1970S. The design of this advertisement to promote police-community relations originated in Minneapolis and was used through the country in the early 1970s. This sign was placed at Woodward and Jefferson Avenues in January 1971 by Eller Outdoor Advertising Company. The placement was celebrated by the attendance of Mayor Gribbs, and plans were made to place an additional 25 billboards around the city.

DETROIT POLICE ATHLETIC LEAGUE POSTER, 1970. The Detroit Police Athletic League (PAL) and Think Detroit recently underwent a merger and now operate under one new name: Think Detroit PAL. One of the purposes of this partnership between the department and community volunteers is to build character in young people through athletic, academic, and leadership development programs. The organization annually serves more than 13,000 kids with the assistance of over 1,500 volunteers.

THIRD DEPUTY CHIEF RICHARD "NIGHT TRAIN" LANE, 1970. Richard Lane led the National Football League in interceptions twice (1952 and 1954) and was All-Pro five times and a Pro Bowl choice six times. After retiring from football, he became director of the department's police athletic league. In 1974, he was a unanimous selection to the Pro Football Hall of Fame. He passed away in February 2002. He will be remembered not only for his performance on the football field but also for his work with youths in this city.

THE BLUE PIGS ALBUM COVER, 1970S. During the summer of 1970, Graham Prince, a musical arranger and composer, believed that the department could use music to reach people and promote education. Having had experience with network television and Hollywood studios, he took his idea to Superintendent John Nichols, who loved the idea and gave permission to start the audition process. Superintendent Nichols came up with the original name of the group, Les Cochons Bleus, which is French for "the blue pigs."

BLUE PIGS IN FRONT OF *SPIRIT OF DETROIT* STATUE, 1970S. The Blue Pigs pose in front of the *Spirit of Detroit*, a bronze statue created by Marshall Fredericks and located on the west end of the Coleman A. Young Municipal Center. As one of Detroit's most easily identifiable landmarks, a sketch of the statue appears as the central element of most of the logos for City of Detroit departments and services. Several years ago a prankster painted green footprints (the color of the statue) leading from the base of the monument to Giacomo Manzu's nude *Passo di Danza* ("step of the dance") bronze sculpture nearby.

THE BIG FOUR, 1971. During the 1960s, the department used what was referred to as the "Big Four," or tac squads, each made up of four officers, to patrol neighborhoods. In the early days, the original teams developed a reputation among the minority residents of Detroit for harassment and brutality. The racial integration of these teams improved the community image of these units. These officers are identified as, from left to right, Dennis Dionne (crew chief), Kenneth Woodruff (driver), "handsome and cool-talking" Dave Bruce, and Willie Peeples.

POLICE OFFICER WILLIAM CUMMINGS, 1971. This photograph shows Officer William Cummings working as a member of the department's Big Four. Officer Cummings went on to obtain his law degree and retire from the department as a commander.

DIVERS, 1971. The Detroit Police Department's Underwater Recovery Team was organized in 1964. It is responsible for all recovery operations conducted in the Detroit River and other bodies of water around the Detroit area. The primary mission of the team is the recovery of physical evidence that has been disposed of in the water. This includes the recovery of bodies, weapons, vehicles, and other items.

DIVERS FLOATING DOWN THE RIVER ON ICE, 1971. Training for the team is conducted twice a month year-round, and divers are on call 24 hours a day and must respond even in the harsh winter months. When members are not diving they are assigned to various patrol functions within the department. The two divers are identified as Sergeants Gary Snyder (left) and John Ronan.

DETROIT POLICE DEPARTMENT DIVER, 1971. Membership on the team is strictly on a voluntary basis and is limited to sworn members. Applicants are required to hold the minimum of an Advanced Open Water Certification for consideration to the team. Applicants must also pass a rigorous physical and swim test before final acceptance to the team. Sergeant Robert Wolfe, one of a crack team of eight police divers, is shown here making a practice dive in the Detroit River.

HARBORMASTER BOAT, 1972. As this photograph reveals, the work of the Harbormaster boat officers was not restricted to fair-weather boating.

DIVER BEING AIRLIFTED TO HOSPITAL, 1978. Emphasizing the work hazards of the scuba diving team, diver James Pallarito is pictured here being airlifted to Hutzel Hospital after receiving an injury during an attempt to recover the bodies of two small children who had drowned in the icy Detroit River on the previous day.

STRESS DECOYS, 1971–1974. In response to an increase in street robberies in 1970, the department created a special unit called Stop the Robberies Enjoy Safe Streets (STRESS). A small number of officers assigned to STRESS were part of a decoy unit that became very controversial during its existence. During its brief tenure, the decoys were involved in 36 shootings, 22 of them fatal. These male officers are dressed in women's clothing for street duty. Newly elected Mayor Coleman A. Young kept his promise to voters to dismantle the unit when he was elected to office.

STELLA OF GREEKTOWN, 1970S. For many years, Stella, a homeless lady, was an iconic figure for the officers assigned to Detroit Police Headquarters and the shopkeepers in the surrounding Greektown area. Stella spent many a night sleeping on the wooden bench in the First Precinct station. On any given day, her personal laundry could be found on a makeshift clothesline between the headquarters building and the jail. Officers routinely provided her with police paraphernalia that she meticulously maintained, such as a nightstick, lieutenant's bars, sergeant's chevrons, lapel pins, tie tacks, patches, and so on. The Detroit Police Mounted patch is sewn onto the clothing on her right arm. Although Stella was clearly never an official member of the department, apparently the close contact with law enforcement honed her criminal investigation skills. One day she alerted the First Precinct officers of an intruder in the basement of headquarters and the suspect was immediately taken into custody. Stella got her man.

DOROTHY D. KNOX, HALL OF HONOR, 1973. This photograph was taken during the department's annual firearms qualifications by a *Detroit News* photographer. Dorothy D. Knox was one of several women in the department who were able to pass through the glass ceiling. In 1986, she became one of the first women to be promoted to commander and was put in charge of the Community Services Division. A few years later, she was promoted to deputy chief. She is one of the many successful women who are listed in the Criminal Justice and Law Center's Hall of Honor posted by Lansing Community College.

SHOWING THE SOFTER SIDE OF POLICING, EARLY 1970S. Police officers have been referred to as an "anomaly in a free society" because of the conflicting roles they play. On the one hand, they are expected to be very tough and restrain people who are out of control, arrest them if necessary, and even use serious force in extreme cases. On the other hand, they are expected to be concerned, patient, caring, and compassionate individuals. These series of pictures reveal the soft, compassionate side of policing. These officers are assigned to the Tactical Mobile Unit that sponsored annual picnics for busloads of handicapped children that included amusement park rides, clowns, rides in patrol cars, scooters, ponies, and of course eating hot dogs. Officer Armand Watson is shown here pushing Brian Sherman on a swing while Sergeant Lawrence Van Alstine is having a great time with Lennie Carpenter on the merry-go-round.

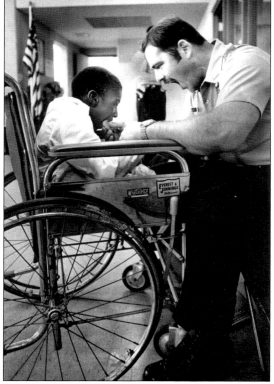

TACTICAL MOBILE UNIT, EARLY 1970S.
Officer Raymond Smith enjoys a hot dog with Steven Schwartz while Officer Joseph Soloman offers a big bite of a hot dog to Darrel Harvey. It is difficult to determine who is having more fun or who benefits more from these encounters. However, it is likely that it is the officers themselves, since after all, the most often stated reason for entering police work in the first place is to help people. These officers, as well as hundreds of thousands of others, show this each and every day, both on and off the job.

DETROIT POLICE HELICOPTER FLYING OVER DOWNTOWN, 1973. Commissioner Philip G. Tannian and pilot Donald Camden return after a tour of the downtown area of Detroit in one of four new helicopters put into service by the Detroit Police Department. The chopper, a 1973 Bell 4705A, is fitted with a 3.8 million–candlepower searchlight.

CREATION OF THE BOARD OF POLICE COMMISSIONERS, 1974. Created in 1974, a five-member civilian Board of Police Commissioners was vested supervisory authority over the department. Mayor Coleman A. Young convened the first meeting on July 24, 1974. Pictured from left to right are Commissioner Edward J. Littlejohn, Commissioner Alexander B. Ritchie (vice chairperson), Commissioner Susan Mills-Peek, Mayor Coleman A. Young, Commissioner Douglas Fraser, James Bradley (city clerk), Commissioner Reverend Charles Butler (chairperson), and Chief Philip Tannian.

BOARD OF POLICE COMMISSIONERS FULFILLS MANDATE, 1980. Six years after its inception, the Board of Police Commissioners took control of the citizen complaint process. Three members of the board with two members of their staff are pictured here. From left to right are Chief Investigator Odson Tetreault, Executive Secretary David F. Smydra, Commissioner Sharon Miller, Commissioner Walter Douglas, and Commissioner Reverend Malcolm Carron. Not present were Commissioner S. Martin Taylor and Commissioner Eugene Driker. The artwork on the wall was by Sergeant John Rau of the department's Graphic Arts Unit.

GRADUATING CLASS, EARLY 1974. This was the first time that women officers outnumbered men in a Detroit recruit training class. Of the 70 graduates, 39 were women. Shortly after this picture was taken, the skirts were turned in for regular uniform pants. Officers Carol Doench and Susan Anderson were following in their fathers' footsteps by joining the force. Officer Lerendeen Smith (first officer on the right) would eventually become an executive in the department and commanding officer of police personnel.

WOMEN ASSIGNED TO REGULAR PATROL, 1974. In 1974, the Women's Division of the department, where all female officers had previously been assigned once completing the recruit training academy, was dissolved. For the first time in its history, the department began assigning females to regular patrol duties. Officer Brenda Milliken was among the first female officers assigned to precinct duties.

DETROIT POLICE CADET PROGRAM, 1975. Students at Chadsey High School and Miller Junior High School participated in a summer police cadet program sponsored by the Detroit Police Department, the board of education, and the In-School Neighborhood Youth Corp. Girls were included for the first time this year. One of the functions performed by police cadets is to assist the elderly with various tasks. Since its inception, the young volunteers of the cadet program have donated thousands of hours to community service.

HOW TALL IS TALL ENOUGH, 1975. Sanshiro Miyamoto was three inches too short to meet the five-foot-eight-inch height requirements in 1972. He even went as far as having his wife hit him over the head with a board so his head would swell an additional half inch. His plight came to national attention when he appeared on the Johnny Carson show on August 15, 1972. Although he gave up his efforts, his even-shorter younger brother, Akiyo, was subsequently hired when Commissioner Philip Tannian abolished all height requirements. Here Akiyo Miyamoto poses with another recruit, John Matchulat, who towers above him.

THE LIVERNOIS-FENKELL CIVIL
DISTURBANCE, 1975. Officer Denise Halloran
and her squad leader, Sergeant Jack Curry,
are standing at the ready in response to the
eruption of violence and civil unrest that was
preceded by the killing of a youth at a local
bar. Newly elected Mayor Coleman A. Young
has been credited with quelling the violence by
his appearance in the area for several evenings
after the initial incident. His actions were a
testimonial to his leadership of the city for the
next two decades.

FEMALE ROOKIES ON PATROL, 1976. Initially some of the female officers were not enthusiastic
about being assigned to patrol duties. However, many of the officers, including Officers Joann
Wilson, Mary Sihler, and Laurie Soper pictured here one year later, relished the idea.

FEMALE OFFICER WITH RENAISSANCE CENTER IN BACKGROUND, 1977. This unidentified officer is photographed with the Renaissance Center in the background. The center was built in 1976, just before this picture was taken. The structure is 73 stories high, and one of the towers houses General Motors headquarters.

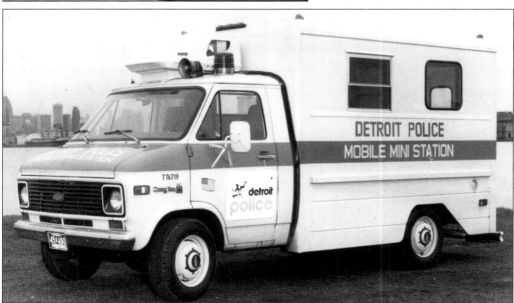

MOBILE MINI-STATION, 1977. In 1974, the Mini-Station program was implemented with the opening of 15 new mini-precincts in the city. Staffed by regular patrol officers and volunteer citizens, the program became so successful that the department put these mobile Mini-Stations into use. The concept was to target neighborhoods that were experiencing high crime rates. The program's continued success resulted in nearly 50 Mini-Stations being in operation by 1979. The Mini-Station concept became a model for law enforcement agencies around the country.

"WELCOME TO OUR NEIGHBORHOOD," 1974. In a show of support, neighborhood children greeted the officers assigned to the Herman Gardens Mini-Station with these drawings welcoming them to the neighborhood. This is just one testimonial of the effectiveness of the Mini-Station concept.

STOLEN POLICE DOG RETURNED TO OFFICER, 1976. On September 28, 1976, King was "dog-napped" from the back of a police cruiser while it was parked in the Greektown area of Detroit. Many police departments train their dogs in the aggressive "bite and hold" method, but Detroit Police Department canines receive training in the nonaggressive "bark and hold" method. The photograph shows King being reunited with his partner, Officer Leonard Riccinto. The search for King was extensive and even included a helicopter search. Police received more than 100 tips and were able to recover King without incident.

BOMB SQUAD VAN AND TRAILER, 1980S. Many departments, including federal agencies, have molded their bomb-disposal units after the Detroit Police Department Bomb Squad.

TACTICAL SERVICES SECTION, 1978. By the late 1970s, the Tactical Services Section, formerly known as the Tactical Mobile Unit, had become the primary unit to handle situations that required special weapons or tactics.

TACTICAL SERVICES SQUAD NO. 2, 1978. Officers of the Tactical Services Section regularly received advanced training so that they were prepared to respond to serious situations.

EVIDENCE TECHNICIAN OFFICER, 1978. In 1968, the department began training evidence technicians to respond to various crime scenes and collect evidence.

EVIDENCE GUNS, 1982. Officer James Prill displays a small derringer and a pistol with an assortment of numerous shotguns and long guns in the background. These weapons represent more than 25,000 firearms stored in the Detroit Police Department's property room. In 1982, the police department made 3,327 arrests of persons unlawfully carrying a weapon. In the same year, the police department's crime laboratory section examined 5,663 pieces of firearms evidence (guns, spent bullets, and casings) for presentation in court proceedings.

DISPATCHING CARS, 1978. Communications Operations is responsible for the efficient operation of the dispatching and messaging center for the Detroit Police Department, and it plays a vital role in relaying information, not just within the city but also between Detroit and the surrounding cities and counties. Emergency calls are received here and relayed to officers on the street. This photograph shows Officer Michael Jastremski sitting in front of his complex communications console at police headquarters.

NEW MOBILE DATA TERMINAL, 1977. By 1977, technological advances in communications provided the department with the opportunity to acquire the new mobile data terminals (MDT) and install them in patrol vehicles. These computers allowed officers to have ready access to information on wanted persons and vehicles, allowing them to run checks from their cars rather than contacting the dispatcher over the police radio.

KEYSTONE KOPS WITH TROLLEY, 1979. The Keystone Kops were a complement to the trolley that ran on Washington Boulevard at that time. While they acted to promote police-community relations, they also performed the regular functions of foot patrol officers.

KEYSTONE KOPS, 1979. As part of a community relations effort, on June 22, 1977, Detroit police officers assigned to the First Precinct began to walk a Washington Boulevard beat dressed in vintage 1910 police uniforms that consisted of a long, navy blue jacket with a single row of brass buttons and an egg-shaped helmet, but their guns and walkie-talkies, or PREP radios, were a reminder that they were modern officers. In this photograph, Officers Felix Kirk and Frank Nazar greet children who are fascinated with the uniforms.

FIRST FEMALE PRECINCT COMMANDER, 1981. Over time, as more women joined the department, they stepped into roles previously held only by male officers. Inspector Billie Willis, a former member of the Women's Division seen here with her clerk, became the first female in the history of the department to command a precinct.

NARCOTICS PATCH, 1983. The dedicated officers assigned to narcotics enforcement in the department enforce laws relating to illegal drugs by conducting surveillance of drug dealers and working undercover to infiltrate drug organizations. In addition, the officers have carried out raids in thousands of locations and confiscated millions of dollars in narcotics, weapons, and cash. One of their primary goals is to reduce the sources of dangerous drugs on the street.

BREAKING THE GLASS CEILING, 1986. In 1986, Commander Mary Jarrett-Jackson was promoted to the rank of deputy chief. At that time, it made her the highest-ranking female officer since the department had reorganized in 1974. Coincidentally, Deputy Chief Jarrett-Jackson made news just three years earlier when she was the first female to be promoted to the rank of commander.

WORLD CHAMPION TUG-OF-WAR TEAM, 1987. Detroit's finest once again won the annual tug-of-war contest with the Windsor Police Department. The Detroit officers stood in Hart Plaza, in the city of Detroit, and the Canadians stood in Dieppe Park in the city of Windsor. The rope was stretched across the river between them. Glory went to the first team to pull 1,000 feet of the rope, which was anchored in the Detroit River.

POLICE EXPLORERS GRADUATION, 1987. The Police Explorers program began in 1972, with the idea of giving youth an inside look at, and fresh perspective on, the day-to day operations of the department. These young people travel the country on a volunteer basis and participate in competitions that demonstrate their knowledge of law enforcement. The Detroit Explorer post holds several local and national competitive titles.

ROBOCOP IN FRONT OF 2110 PARK STREET, 1987. Neither the Detroit Police Department nor the city of Detroit are typically thought of as setting the stage for Hollywood motion pictures. However, there have been several notably successful movies such as *Beverly Hills Cop*, *Assault on Precinct 13*, and of course *Robocop*, the lead actor of which is seen in this photograph standing next to his Detroit police patrol car.

MAYOR YOUNG ADDRESSES POLICE OFFICERS REHIRED AFTER LAYOFFS, 1981. City budget cuts forced the layoff of hundreds of police officers, many of whom were laid off up to five years. Here Mayor Coleman A. Young welcomes a group of recalled officers.

AERIAL VIEW OF THE CITY, 1989. Police helicopters routinely fly over the city as support units for patrol officers on the ground. They can provide aerial surveillance, methodically follow criminals, and make emergency flights to hospitals. The Detroit Police Air Patrol Bureau was established in 1948. The personnel assigned to the bureau consisted of one police officer who owned and operated a fixed wing airplane (a Vultee BT-13). In 1971, the Aviation Section was reinitiated with the addition of helicopters.

Six

CONTINUING TO MAKE HISTORY

A VISIT FROM NELSON MANDELA, 1990. Nelson Mandela made a visit to the United States in June 1990, after his release from 27 years of imprisonment in South Africa. It was a visit that brought a tremendous outpouring of emotion and support at every stop.

CELEBRITIES LISTENING TO MANDELA'S INSPIRATION, 1990. Rosa Parks and federal judge Damon Keith were two of the many celebrities in attendance at Nelson Mandela's speech. It is reported that while walking to the podium Nelson Mandela stopped in front of Rosa Parks and said "you were my inspiration while I was in prison all of those years."

MANDELA'S MOTORCADE AND DONNING A DETROIT PISTONS NBA CHAMPIONSHIP JACKET, 1990. During his visit, Nelson Mandela spoke of peace and unity and offered heartfelt congratulations to the NBA champions, the Detroit Pistons.

McGruff the Crime Dog, 1992. McGruff the Crime Dog and his slogan "Take a Bite Out of Crime" were a creation of the National Advertising Council. The Detroit Police Department's McGruff is one of over 4,000 official McGruffs nationwide. Over the years, McGruff has made thousands of appearances at community and school events and on radio and television. From schoolchildren to senior citizens, McGruff promotes safety and crime prevention. In 1984, the U.S. Postal Service even released a first-class postage stamp bearing McGruff's likeness.

Even Officers Need a Break, 1994. Because their jobs often require responding at a moment's notice, police officers know the value of a coffee break. Officers will often carry with them reminders of loved ones who are tucked in safely at home while they patrol the streets.

THEN AND NOW, 1994. In 1994, Inspector Robert Williams wrote an article titled "Then and Now" depicting the tradition of innovation in the Detroit Police Department and highlighting the Detroit Emergency Response System (DETERS). This system, developed in cooperation with the University of Michigan Studies in Urban Security, enabled the department to reduce the amount of time it took to respond to emergency situations. When introduced in April 1989, it was the first and only one of its kind. By 1994, police departments all over the world were once again duplicating what the Detroit Police Department had created.

OLD AND NEW - The 1940 Ford DeLuxe Detroit cruiser (left) sported a flathead V-8 engine. The 1993 Crown Victoria cruiser (right) has a 4.6-liter, V-8 electronically controlled automatic overdrive transmission producing 210 horsepower.

DETERS
DETROIT EMERGENCY RESPONSE SYSTEM

By Robert Earl Williams
Inspector, Detroit Police

The City of Detroit has long been a proving ground for new emergency technologies from the first radio dispatch in 1928 to the early MDT in the 1970s.

Following in that tradition of innovation, city personnel worked with the University of Michigan's Studies in Urban Security group to design the DEtroit Emergency Response System (DETERS). This system was developed to help reduce the time it takes to respond to emergencies and improve the quality of our emergency service.

When introduced to the world in April of 1989, this system was the first and only one of its kind in the United States. Today, cities across the world are duplicating this system.

DETERS encompasses five main components:

MOBILE DIGITAL RADIO. The system begins with this link in Detroit's emergency response network, which provides an unbreakable connection between dispatch personnel and 9-1-1 callers. As a 9-1-1 call is received, the system automatically displays the precise origin of the call, including the address and the name of the person to whom the call is billed. Enhanced 9-1-1 "holds" the line open until the dispatcher voluntarily releases it.

COMPUTER AIDED DISPATCH (CAD). This link of DETERS accepts and utilizes the E9-1-1 information and keeps all of the master records of the entire system. In effect, it ties all of the other systems together. CAD contains the geobase file that identifies the source of the call, provides it to the dispatcher's graphic workstation and recommends what it believes is the best response - for example, which emergency vehicles to send on any given call. CAD also alerts the dispatcher when a vehicle is overdue after responding to a call.

The wealth of information amassed by this city about its structures, streets and utilities can be accessed instantly by Detroit's emergency-response dispatchers via CAD. For example, law enforcement personnel who must enter a building under potentially dangerous circumstances can reduce their "unknowns" when CAD provides pertinent information on the address and its owner - such as whether a house has a known history of drug activity. In another application, the city's existing data base on hazardous materials can be accessed to warn firefighters immediately when such substances are known to be stored at the scene of a fire. *To Page 70*

DEPARTMENT EXECUTIVES CAN SING TOO, 1990S. From left to right, Deputy Chief Nathaniel Topp, Commander Fred Campbell, Deputy Chief Rudy Thomas, Deputy Chief Daniel McKane, Lieutenant James Zachary, and Chief Isaiah McKinnon belt out a holiday song for the troops at the annual office Christmas party.

SUPERBOWL XL IN THE MOTOR CITY, 2006. The 2005–2006 football season came to a wondrous finale in Detroit with the Pittsburgh Steelers winning the championship for the first time in 20 years. Nearly a million people flooded the downtown area to celebrate. Even the *Spirit of Detroit* showed its support.

The Blackout, 2003. In 2003, the department's true test to serve and protect was challenged in the darkness of what was called the largest blackout in North American history. Detroit police officers answered the call and defended the city.

CRIMINAL JUSTICE INSTITUTE
CLASS 77-O

ACADEMY CLASS 77-O, 1977. The recruit training class 77-O included Ella M. Bully. In the 1980s, she was among hundreds of police officers who were laid off due to budget constraints. She returned to the department in 1985 and went on to graduate cum laude from Michigan State University College of Law and was sworn into the State Bar of Michigan in May 1998. In 2002, after working several years as an attorney, she was called back to the department by Mayor Kwame M. Kilpatrick and appointed as the first female assistant chief of police in the department's history. In November 2003, Mayor Kilpatrick appointed her as the department's first female chief of police in its 138-year history.

SCHOOL DAYS, 2003. As always, the Detroit Police Department remains committed to the children of the city it serves. These photographs show officers from Special Events, a unit designed to coordinate and oversee all major events that occur within the city of Detroit. The officers guide the children through the functioning and use of their equipment. Officers recognize that by reaching out to the children early, they may promote a more solid community partnership later on.

THANKSGIVING DAY PARADE, 2004. Chief Ella M. Bully-Cummings walks with local area children in the 2004 Thanksgiving Day parade. Each year, this event draws hundreds of thousands of people and their families from all over southeast Michigan. They line Woodward Avenue and gaze upon the fun-filled and colorful floats that most only get to see on television.

HONOR GUARD MARCHES IN PARADE, 2004. Shown here is the Detroit Police Honor Guard displaying flags in the Thanksgiving Day parade. Behind the guard is the Fox Theater, which was built in 1928 and was the first movie palace to have live sound. It was designated a national historic landmark in 1989.

Rosa Parks, Going Home Ceremony, 2005. In 1957, at the urging of her brother and sister-in-law, Rosa Parks, her husband Raymond, and her mother Leona McCauley moved to Detroit. Rosa worked as a seamstress until 1965 when African American U.S. Representative John Conyers hired her as a secretary and receptionist for his congressional office in Detroit. She held this position until she retired in 1988. On August 30, 1994, a man named Joseph Skipper attacked 81-year-old Rosa in her home. The incident sparked outrage throughout America. An investigation by the department revealed that Skipper had not known he was in Rosa's home at first but recognized her after entering. Skipper asked, "Hey, aren't you Rosa Parks?" to which she replied, "Yes." She handed him $3 when he demanded money, and an additional $50 when he demanded more. Before fleeing, Skipper struck Rosa in the face. Skipper was arrested and charged with a variety of offenses against Rosa and other neighborhood victims. He admitted guilt and on August 8, 1995, was sentenced to 8 to 15 years in prison.

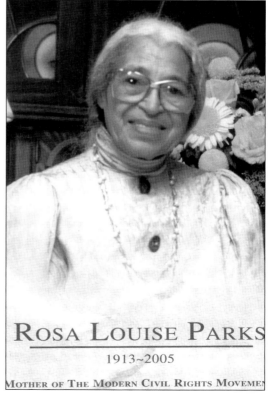

ROSA LOUISE PARKS

1913~2005

MOTHER OF THE MODERN CIVIL RIGHTS MOVEMEN

"Detroit's Finest Hour"
Hurricane Relief Fundraiser

November 18, 2005

6:30pm - 9:00pm

Masonic Temple Fountain Ballroom
Detroit, Michigan
USA

The Honorable Kwame M. Kilpatrick
Mayor, City of Detroit

Ella M. Bully-Cummings
Chief of Police

KATRINA CHARITY BENEFIT, ONE OF DETROIT'S FINEST HOURS, 2005. In August 2005, Hurricane Katrina, one of the five deadliest hurricanes on record, hit the state of Louisiana, killing 1,836 people. Within hours, Detroit police officers, volunteering their own time, made their way to the devastated area to assist in rescue attempts. In November, officers that could not spend time in New Orleans lent their voices by way of a charity concert called Detroit's Finest Hour. The benefit raised several thousand dollars, which was donated to the relief fund.

DETROIT SWAT, 2006. The Detroit Special Response Team (SRT) was profiled in a reality television program on the A&E Network called *Detroit SWAT.* It first aired in 2006, giving viewers a look into the day-to-day operations of the unit. The Detroit SRT was organized in 1987 and deployed on its first mission in April 1988. During that first mission, Officer Frank Walls and Lieutenant James Schmidt were killed by a barricaded gunman. Since then, Detroit SRT holds one of the lowest fatality rates in the country for special response units by adhering to a strict negotiation policy before deploying tactical action.

DETROIT OFFICERS RIDE ON BELLE ISLE, 2008. Chief Ella M. Bully-Cummings poses with motor officers of the Traffic Enforcement Unit during the 100th anniversary celebration of the partnership between Harley-Davidson and the Detroit Police Department.

DETROIT POLICE CELEBRATE 100 YEARS WITH HARLEY-DAVIDSON, 2008. June 2008 marked the Detroit Police Department's 100-year partnership with Harley-Davidson. The motor officers of the department's Traffic Enforcement Unit held a bike ride and rally on Belle Isle to celebrate.

THE DETROIT POLICE CHAPLIN CORPS, 2008. The first three chaplains of the Detroit Police Department were appointed in 1949 by Commissioner Henry S. Toy. They became full members of the department with gold badges and identification cards. However, the Chaplain Corps was not established until 1974 and was made official by city ordinance on January 28, 1975. The corps offers spiritual guidance and counsel to officers, employees, and their families. Detroit police chaplains serve without remuneration.

HONORING FALLEN HEROES, 2008. In April 2008, the Detroit Police Honor Guard presented the colors at a ceremony to honor the 214 Detroit officers who had given their lives to serve and protect their citizens.

CHIEF BULLY-CUMMINGS ADDRESSES THE TROOPS, 2008. At a dedication ceremony held for fallen Detroit police officers, Chief Ella M. Bully-Cummings addresses the troops to thank them for their service and to pay homage to those who have made the ultimate sacrifice.

A 21-GUN SALUTE IN HONOR OF DETROIT'S FALLEN OFFICERS. In honoring fallen officers, funereal customs follow military tradition and often include the honor of a 21-gun salute, which is somewhat of a misnomer since, in practice, it involves the firing of three volleys from seven rifles, as shown here.

THE MEMORIAL WALL, 2008. To honor fallen Detroit police officers, the Detroit Police Foundation dedicated this wall with each fallen officer's name and photograph.

DETROIT POLICE DEPARTMENT BUGLER PLAYING TAPS. Every police officer recognizes the haunting but eloquent melody of taps that is played at the funerals, wreath-layings, and memorial services for fallen officers.

Dedicated to Detroit police officers, past, present, and future.

ACROSS AMERICA, PEOPLE ARE DISCOVERING SOMETHING WONDERFUL. *THEIR HERITAGE.*

Arcadia Publishing is the leading local history publisher in the United States. With more than 3,000 titles in print and hundreds of new titles released every year, Arcadia has extensive specialized experience chronicling the history of communities and celebrating America's hidden stories, bringing to life the people, places, and events from the past. To discover the history of other communities across the nation, please visit:

www.arcadiapublishing.com

Customized search tools allow you to find regional history books about the town where you grew up, the cities where your friends and family live, the town where your parents met, or even that retirement spot you've been dreaming about.